Community Leadership Handbook

PREPARING

TO RUN

FOR LOCAL

OFFICE

GARY DAVIS

Preparing to Run for Local Office

First Edition, July 4, 2021

This book is designed to provide information and motivation to readers. It is sold with the understanding that the author is not engaged to render any type of legal or expert advice. The content of this book is the sole expression and opinion of its author. You are responsible for your own choices, actions, and results.

ISBN: 9798524522832

Printed in the United States of America

CONTENTS

First, the numbers:

There are over **40,000 municipal governments**, **14,000 school districts**, and **38,000 special districts** in the United States. Over **600,000 board members** govern these **92,000 local districts**. These leaders help direct the trillions of dollars annually affecting the over **330 million United States residents.**

Someone is elected to these boards every election cycle. **Why shouldn't that someone be you?**

Introduction

My name is Gary Davis. Born and raised in a suburban middle-class community, my dad worked for the State of California for 40 years and retired. My mom was a full-time volunteer, giving her time and energy to a number of local community groups. Looking back, it's clear that my interest in public service, giving back to the community, came from the example my mom set for me. I had a drive in me to become something - to make a real difference in life. Heading into college as a business major, I had one goal - get a job in corporate America, climb the ladder, and get rich. That all changed my Junior year when I took a women's studies course. In that class, we were discussing that the student government would vote to shut down the Women's Resource Center on campus - a move that seemed incredibly ill-conceived and just not fair or right. We reacted like many college students did, by picketing and protesting. We mobilized quite an army of people to storm the student government chambers during the vote. We advocated. We had large numbers. We made highly effective arguments. But we lost the vote.

It was at that moment where I had a decision to make. I could walk away and know that I tried this advocacy thing, but that it wasn't for me. Perhaps I would continue to focus on trying to climb the corporate ladder. Or I could pivot entirely and take it to the next level by running for office myself - gaining both a voice and a vote on the other side of that dais. That's exactly what I did. The person who had spearheaded the effort to close the Women's Resource Center was the Student Body President, who had run for reelection. So, I ran against her, winning the election by 4 votes. Yes, 4 votes! I can affirm that, literally, every vote counts.

At this same time in College, 1997, I was selected to be part of the Sacramento Entrepreneurship Academy, a one-year program where we convened every Saturday for a year to learn about starting a business. In the Academy, we formed teams to research and write a business plan for a new company. Together, our team of four developed a business idea and wrote a business plan. At the end of the year, we presented our business plan to a group of venture capitalists and successful entrepreneurs. Our idea, an online restaurant reservation software platform, was praised at the presentation for having viability in what was then a new and up and coming world of the internet. The four of us, however, all had different plans and none of us pursued the business. To be clear, this was exactly one year BEFORE the guy who invented OpenTable had his idea. That guy launched OpenTable and later sold it for $4 billion. So, as it turns out, I really could have been rich had I stayed on my original path. My calling, however, was higher.

After college, I moved to a new city and immediately became engaged and involved in the civic fabric of the community. Within just a few months, I had recruited two other people and the three of us challenged three long-time incumbents on the local school board. It was the perfect battle. Us three challengers vs. the three incumbents. We won all three seats and gained an instant majority of the board. At the end of my 4-year term, we moved to another city. Again, I immediately got involved in the civic fabric of the community. Within a matter of months, I found myself challenging the incumbent City Councilman in a high stakes, expensive, campaign. I beat him by 21 points. I later became my city's first directly elected Mayor - the best job in the world in my opinion.

In 2016, I decided not to seek reelection and instead focus on my family and career. Now, I get to help other people navigate their path to community leadership and help people like you achieve your dreams within your community. I have coached over 350 candidates for elected office and presented to hundreds more about how to become community involved and engaged in their community. I love it! Being engaged in your community is positively one of the most rewarding things a person can do and, arguably, is where you have the biggest opportunity to impact real change in the lives of people. I hope you, too, get bit by the local community service bug and follow the outline in this handbook. You won't regret it.

Preface

All politics, and therefore advocacy, is local.
Whether or not you seek to influence your local
school board, city council, state legislature, or the
United States Congress, it is the local issues that
impact people daily. Every elected official is hired
by their local community and every elected official
can be fired by the same people. If your schools
are terrible, crime is high, and potholes aren't
filled, the bigger, more partisan, issues don't
matter as much to people day-to-day. Effective
politicians first take care of their local issues.
Doing so, they build a solid community foundation
on which to stand to fight for the larger state or
national issues.

As a potential community leader and advocate, a
mastery of local issues will position you to get
beyond the isolated bubble you may be living in
and build bridges that lead to coalitions of support.
When you show up at a public meeting by yourself
to advocate for a position, politicians barely look

up at you. If you pack the house with a multitude of people from different geographies, groups, and interests, they pay attention. If you can bring together a large and diverse coalition of community leaders and organizations, including people who are unexpected, politicians come your way. It's just the way it is and has been since the beginning of time.

The goal of this handbook is to provide you with simple, common sense, tools to become more interconnected to the civic fabric of your community - raising your personal community profile along the way. After reading this handbook, you will reflect on the simple, common sense, nature of the ideas we discussed. Yet, the formula I will share with you is full of insider tricks and tips. If you implement this formula, you will become a community influencer. People will look to you to lead them in your community. If you run for office, you can be positioned as a front-runner from the day you announce your candidacy. If you use these skills to advocate on an important issue, decision-makers will take notice. You will change your community.

The secondary goal of this handbook is to prepare you to run for elected office, should you choose to do so. If you follow the formula laid out in this handbook, before telling people of your intention to run for office, you will significantly raise your personal community profile. I call this the "pre-campaign" period. Most people who run for office don't do a "pre-campaign." They rarely win the first time around. The "pre-campaign" is the time between when you decide to run for office and the time when you tell others you will run. Once you decide to run, you will be tempted to tell everyone, but don't do it. If you follow the steps in the handbook and run your "pre-campaign" effectively, your campaign will launch with such momentum you will be hard to beat. This is the secret sauce you now have access to the ingredients because you picked up this handbook.

1
HARNESSING MY
EXPERIENCE

Let's start with a little introspection and look inward at who you are and what makes you unique. Knowing first who you are and what you believe, will provide a game plan of who could be your natural allies as you begin to build bridges and make community connections. For just about every characteristic you can possibly have, there is likely someone or some organization just like you – that wants to partner with you and is vested in your success. These are often people or organizations with immense political clout and you have an obvious connection to them. Examples include:

- Women's groups that want to help other women become community leaders.
- Ethnic groups that want to see more of their own people elected to political office.
- Trade associations who need like-minded people in leadership positions.

Below please find an
exercise called Identify
Circles. Several versions of
this exercise, including a
version often used for team
building, bring participants
to tears (I won't do that to
you). As you approach this
exercise, try and frame your
mind around a community
lens. Yes - the exercise is
about you and you should include your very
personal traits, identity, and characteristics;
however, deliberately contemplate which
identifying factor you hold that would endear you
to the community around you.

Start by putting your name in the middle of the
sun. Around the sun are a number of triangles, or
sun rays. Off of each sun ray, list something that is
important to your identity. These traits could

include race, identification, gender, hobbies, political party, or other interests. Examples could include being Asian, religious, an artist, LGTBQ, a parent, business owner, union member, and much more.

Take at least 15 minutes to do this exercise and think deeply about what makes you unique and who you are. Don't hold back. You are the only one who needs to see this.

Did you learn anything new about yourself? Did you find yourself afraid or proud to think about yourself? Are you surprised at how diverse you are?

Here is the thing. In politics and community leadership, there is an organization for just about every trait you could possibly have. If you wear their hat, you have a natural affinity to connect with these groups and forge friendships, build coalitions, leverage their power structure, or raise funds. Later we'll take you through an exercise to identify these specific groups and leaders. If you run for office, this is who will play a major role in your base-building outreach. These are also potential partners for advocacy work. Effective advocates can bring key leaders and groups to the table to join their cause, even when there isn't natural issue alignment. Your goal is to build these bridges on a personal level so that they will stand with you and policy makers will pay attention when the time comes.

In the table below, please find just a few organizations you may find a natural affiliation with.

Organization	Mission
Emily's List	Supports pro-choice, women political candidates
Hispanas Organized for Political Equity	Benefits Latinas via leadership, advocacy and education
Emerge California	Develop registered Democratic women running for office
Leadership For Educational Equity (LEE)	Supports diverse leaders with Teach For America backgrounds to engage civically
New American Leaders	Candidate training program targeted for recent American citizens
Association of Realtors	Develop and support Realtor friendly political candidates
The Leadership Institute	Train Conservative candidates for political office
Veterans Campaign	Develop and support military veteran candidates
Victory Institute	Supports LGBTQ candidates

2
DEVELOPING
YOUR STORY

Building off who you are, let's dig a little deeper and craft your personal public narrative. Your public narrative is the "why" of organizing. Learning how to tell your story itself is a leadership skill. I am talking about the skill of telling stories that tap into people's values (rather than just issues) and evoke emotions that move people from inaction to action - emotions of hope, anger, urgency, solidarity, and a sense we can make a difference.

A great example of a deeply personal speech that has affected millions of people is *Steve Jobs 2005 Stanford University Commencement Address*. First, the speech was short. It only lasted 15 minutes. A lot of powerful messages have been delivered in under 18 minutes. John F. Kennedy inspired a nation in 15 minutes and Martin Luther King shared a vision of racial equality in 17 minutes. The speech's meaningful theme resonates with just about everyone who seeks to make a difference in their life and career. There were three main stories - all having deep personal meaning to Jobs. The speech emphasized triumph over adversity. It inspires us to be better.

Your story is the foundation for the rest of your advocacy and leadership work. When you meet another community leader, your story is how you meaningfully connect to them. It becomes the substance of your initial conversations and what makes you memorable to them after you walk away. If you share your story successfully, these community leaders will want to then share it with others and become part of your journey. Not only will they want to be part of your story, but they'll connect you to other community leaders and want them to hear your story and get to know you. Should you run for office in the future, your story also serves as the foundation for all the many forms of your message and your campaign collateral. Your personal story will guide the development of your stump speech, elevator pitch, website, walking brochure, candidate ballot statement, mailers, digital advertising, media messages, and more. It's important to spend time getting it right early on, but also know that your message will likely evolve over time as you tell it over and over and connect with people. You'll get an intuitive sense of what components of your story are particularly meaningful to others and what parts move them and what parts fall flat. Let's look at an example of how not to craft your story. In 1980, Senator Ted Kennedy ran for President of the United States. On all accounts, he was a brilliant politician. He was known for his great oratory skills and came from a deeply experienced political family. Asked on a national news program, in 1979, why he wanted to be President, you can hear his long pause and then two minutes of rambling about issues, but he never answered what should have been the most basic question. Such a softball question should have been a home run for an experienced politician like Senator Kennedy. Look it up on YouTube and see what I mean. Now, let's talk about the right way.

Head & Heart

Each of us have stories that can move others. As you learn this skill of public narrative, you can take stories from your life, from your audience's history, and from whatever issue is facing us, and structure these into a compelling story.

Effective leaders employ both the "head" and the "heart" to mobilize others to act effectively on behalf of our shared values. They engage people in interpreting why they should change the world -

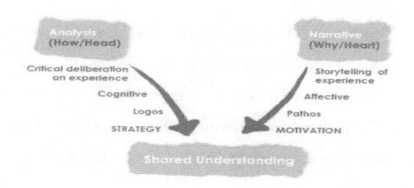

their motivation, and how they can change it - their strategy.

Consider this diagram. The first input is the **How (Head).** This is the specifics of your strategy and how you intend to achieve what you are talking about.

The second input is the **Why (Heart).** This is why something should be important to your audience. It is where you lay out their and your motivation for caring about what you are discussing.

When you can take the "how" of your story and combine it with "why" your audience should care, you reach a **shared understanding** with your audience - you move them to action. Moving your audience to action is the goal of telling your personal story.

Your story of self expresses the values or experiences that call you to take leadership on the issues important to you. A key focus is often on Choice Points - moments in our lives when values are formed because of a need to decide and choose a path in the face of great uncertainty. Choice Points are those moments when we realized what decision needed to be made and then acted on it to make a meaningful difference in the world. Examples of Choice Points include: When did you first care about being heard? Learn that you were concerned about kids? Want to ensure every child has access to a high-quality public education? Get inspired by a social justice issue? Choice Points are not only the when, but also the why. What specific choice did you make for your kids? For all kids? For your community? To fight for an issue? To change the world?

How to Craft Your Story?

There is no perfect formula for crafting your story because your story is unique. Personally, I find it best to consider how other people have crafted their stories and use that as a foundation for developing my own. I recommend taking some time to search YouTube for personal stories that inspire you and seem relevant to your path. There are two, in particular, that I recommend you watch.

- The first two minutes of (then) Senator Obama's 2004 DNC Keynote Speech.
- Dr. Steve Perry's, "Celebrating Your Story"

As you view these YouTube videos, consider these key points:

- What did you learn about the person?
- What was their Choice Point?
- What gives their life meaning?
- Who are they as a person?
- What is their life goal?
- What is their "Why"?
- What is their "How"?
- What are they calling you to do?

Now it's time to craft your personal story. Every person's story is unique to them - that is the point - and it will evolve over time. You will learn what works and what doesn't as you attempt to connect with your audience. Though everything may seem relevant to you, quickly you will learn what to cut out to make your story more potent and memorable. Aim for one page.

As you begin the process, there are a few key prompt questions to ask and answer that will get you pretty far down the path toward developing a robust draft.

- What is the change you want to make in the world?
- Why are you called to make that change?
- What specific experiences have shaped your story?
- What specific personal story can you tell that will help others understand why you want to make that change?
- What were the milestones in your life? What positive experiences have helped define who you are?

- What significant events or periods of your life were challenging? What crises have you encountered?
- What did you learn from those periods of your life? How did some of the challenges help define who you are?
- What transitions have you made in your journey? What decisions had the greatest impact on the path you took in your career or life?
- How did these decisions and transitions impact you? What did you learn in the process?
- How did these experiences shape the advocacy work you now do?
- What is the action you want others to now take?

Start by scripting your story here. Once you do so, type it into an electronic file. Each time you tell your story, think about what worked and what didn't. Consider where people were nodding their heads in agreement and where they may have just been nodding off. Again, there is no perfect formula or approach. Your story is unique to you. Now, let's do it.

My Story

_____

_____

_____

_____

_____

_____

_____

3

RAISING MY

COMMUNITY

PROFILE

Now that you have a good handle on what makes you unique and have taken the time to draft your personal story, I will get into the nitty gritty details about how to plug into the civic fabric of your community. I will be sharing practical, bite-sized, nuggets of information you can use to strategically raise your profile. Your mindset must be wrapped around how to break out of your bubble - your current, limited, sphere of influence. Maybe you are active in the PTA, your church, a specific service club or youth sports. That's a great start - but I will get you beyond this limited sphere and plugged into the broader community. The larger your sphere, the greater the influence you will have.

These are insider secrets! The tactics I will share with you work. If you execute these strategies effectively before becoming a candidate for office, you will launch as a frontrunner - or at least be highly viable. If public office isn't your goal, these tactics will help you to become a community leader with extensive knowledge of the power levers in your community and, therefore, influence.

What is Community Leadership?

Merriam-Webster defines "Leadership" as someone with a position, capacity to lead, or someone in the act of leading. I like to think that community leadership means much more and is more like:

- Getting Stuff Done - Leaders are the people who step up and do the work when others are still talking about it.
- Solving Problems - Leaders take the initiative to solve problems and not just complain about them.
- Developing Relationships - Leaders know how to connect with other people.
- Actively Listening - Leaders listen more than they speak.

- Being Present - Leaders are the people who show up early when others sleep in.
- Serving Others - Leaders serve in their community. They aren't afraid to get their hands dirty.
- Implementing/Filling a Need - Leaders can see the problem, visualize a solution, and work proactively to solve it.
- Connecting People - Leaders can connect other people in ways that benefit them both.
- Honesty - Leaders do what they say they will do and hold secrets close to them. They don't gossip.

I like to talk about leadership in three categories:
Grassroots: These are service clubs and community groups, being an advocate, volunteering or leading a service project or community fundraiser.
Positional: Any appointed position with a title. This could be a local committee or commission,

community association, service club board, coach, etc.

Elected: Each community has a number of ways to serve in elected office. Some of these opportunities include school board, city council, county supervisor, community college board, water board, special district, and more.

So how exactly do you become a community leader?

The simple answer to this intimidating question is that 90% of what it takes to be a community leader is to simply show up. Truly, showing up is 90% of the challenge. If you take the time to be strategically present consistently, you will be significantly ahead of the game and 90% of the way to your goal of attaining community influence.

Twice I ran for office successfully, both times defeating incumbents, in two different communities. In both cases, I ran for office only months after moving into the community. Less than two years living in each community, I was on the ballot and defeated incumbents both times - yet no one accused me of being a "Carpetbagger" - someone who moves into a community to run for office. I contend that it is because I immediately got involved in these communities once I moved there. I showed up, connected with people in a meaningful way, plugged into community service, and did the hard work. By the time the election came around, it didn't feel to anyone like I was new to the community.

Here is why. If you show up and work hard, other leaders will welcome you. There is so much work to be done in every community and not enough people who are truly willing to show up, volunteer, follow-up, and work hard. If you show up regularly and genuinely get engaged in the hard work of serving your community, your impact will be felt. Before you know it, you will be a rising star in your community - someone others look to because you are making a big difference. *Word of warning here* - follow through on all you commit to do and only plug into efforts you truly care about. If you don't, you can just as easily develop a reputation as the person who shows up inconsistently, over promises, and under delivers. Don't be that person.

4
5-STEP PLAN FOR WORLD DOMINATION

Now, it's time to outline what I like to call, my 5-step plan for world domination. This is the roadmap for raising your community profile.

Step 1 - Identify Opportunities in Your Community

Every community has dozens and dozens of opportunities to connect with other leaders and meet people. Being strategically smart about showing up in the right places and knowing what to do when you get there is key to your becoming a known commodity. The first step is to put pen to paper and generate a list of specific places you can show up to connect with existing community leaders. You'll soon learn that the same 100 people attend just about every community event and you will become one of them.

This must be a strategic activity - not you just randomly showing up at places all over town. First define the geographic boundary you wish to conquer. If you will run for office, the geographic

28

area is the boundary of the district in which you hope to run. If advocating a cause is your goal, who are the decision-makers you must influence and what areas do they represent? Define your geographic boundaries around the districts in which they are elected or preside over. If your goals are unsure, start with your immediate community. Then, list out every organization and event from within the electoral boundary.

Examples of events/organizations include:

- Town Hall Meetings
- Community Association Meetings
- Service Club Activities (Rotary, Lyons, Optimists)
- Churches, synagogues, mosques, and other places of worship
- PTA Meetings
- Chamber of Commerce Mixers
- Annual Nonprofit Fundraising Dinners & Events

- Annual Community Awards Dinners or Leadership Installation Luncheons
- School Board or City Council Meetings

Step 2 - Grasstops Networking

After you develop the list of events and organizations, then what? Show Up! If it's easier for you, bring a friend and make a fun night out of it. However, the goal in attending these events is to get beyond your friends. The key to successful networking is to meet new people and make an impression. If you attend a community event and spend all your time talking with people you already know - you have failed. If you desire to raise your community profile, you must meet new people and make new connections.

At the event, track down the event organizers or leaders of the organization leading the community event. Tell them how much you are enjoying the event, how wonderful it is, and that you wonder if you can exchange contact information and get together later? Tell them just a little bit about yourself (your brief story), tell them you are wanting to become more involved in the community, and ask if you can pick their brain about their service and what they think the community needs are. However, keep it brief as they are in the middle of leading or working the event itself. Don't be that person who dominates their time while they are busy.

Grasstops Leaders

On a parallel track, develop a comprehensive list of everyone in your strategically targeted geographic area that has a title. This includes elected officials of all offices, appointed commissioners, nonprofit leaders, community organization leaders, sports league heads, business group leaders, pastors, and, literally, anyone with a title. Do not leave anyone out. If they are within your targeted area and have a title, then they are a grasstops leader. Some have more influence than others. However, all of them have some level of notoriety within their spheres of influence. If you have the time, you want to meet them all.

Step 3 - Position Your Leadership

Once your list is developed, begin your "Coffee Listening Tour" - also called the one-on-one. This is your opportunity to connect directly with existing grasstops community leaders, get to know them, and give them an opportunity to get to know you.

If you can, try and get a warm introduction to each person on your list from someone you already know or have met that will introduce you. Otherwise, cold calls work great too. Don't be afraid to reach out via email or call - even if they don't yet know you. You'll find that most community leaders will meet with you if you approach them the right way. For example:

"Hi! My name is Sally. I live in the Spring Lake neighborhood where we are raising our three children. I have decided it is time to get more involved in the community as I look around and have a few concerns. I see that you are already involved in the community and doing great work! Would you be willing to meet me for a cup of coffee so I can pick your brain about your experience as I also seek the best way to get involved?"

-or-

"Hello! My name is Jose and I am part of the Silver Lake Parents Club. I see you are actively engaged in the community and would love to meet you to learn more about what you do and also share a bit about what we are doing. Would you be available for 30-minutes to meet over a cup of coffee?"

Once they respond, pick a place to meet that is convenient for them and plan on at least an hour meeting. I like neighborhood coffee shops. They are inviting, have lots of seating, and create a great environment for meaningful conversation.

The One-on-One: Now that the meeting is set, what will you be talking about?

This is your opportunity to meaningfully connect with someone who is actively engaged in service to their community. I recommend that you first ask them to share their story. Find out where they are from, why they chose to live where they are now, and what inspired them to become involved in the community.

Then, share your story with them - but don't overdo it. You should be able to share your story with them in 5 minutes or less. If they want more detail, they'll ask you. Over time, as you practice it, sharing your story will become easier and more natural. Your goal is to, of course, share your story - but also try to connect it to their experiences or motivations. If you can connect your story to their interests, you will find shared understanding, leading to a meaningful connection. Your story is also what makes you memorable to them. It's how you walk away and they remember you and want to share the interaction with others they know. After you briefly tell your story, your most important job is to listen! Take in everything you hear and identify, from what you hear, the best opportunities for you to engage in service to your community. You will hear lots of potential opportunities. You need to determine the highest and best use of your time to accomplish your goals and then engage in that activity.

Here are a few questions to ask in the one-on-one:

- Tell me about yourself. What is your story?
- What inspires you to be involved in our community?

- What do you see as our community's largest deficiencies?
- If you are considering a run for office, ask for their opinion about the government agency you want to run for. Maybe even ask what they think of the people who lead that agency. Under no circumstances should you tell them you are considering a run for office at this early stage.

Once you have completed a dozen of these meetings - you will know your community intricately. The knowledge you will have gained by having these meetings will be incredible. You'll have a strong sense of who is doing what in your community, its current needs, but also a very good understanding of your community culture. Further, you will have a deep sense of which people are playing leadership roles on a number of issues. You'll also be able to connect people to each other as one person shares a concern and you know another person that is like-minded. A big part of community leadership is simply facilitating connections for people. You will now be prepared for the next step.

Step 4 - Seek Opportunities to Lead

Let's briefly recap. You started off by identifying specific opportunities to engage in your community. You learned the power of showing up, while identifying grasstops community leaders in a strategic way. Then, you began connecting directly with community leaders and cultivating relationships.

These key foundational steps are leading you toward a very important next step: to identify your best opportunity to get involved and make a difference - the thing you want to do to make your community impact. There are many opportunities to serve your community. The key is to identify something that you truly care about. Others will eventually notice if you pursue a cause or initiative but don't genuinely care about it. Another key point is not to say yes to a task - unless you will do the work to follow through to ensure you deliver on that task in an impressive way. As you engage in the community and take on a cause or task, you will quickly develop a reputation - one way or another. We all know the person who agrees to help with everything - but always flakes or drops the ball and has no follow-through. Don't become that person.

On the upside, if you volunteer to help on a project, join a committee, or work a shift and you show up and do the work and do that consistently, then you will quickly develop the reputation for being someone who gets stuff done and can be relied upon. You will become a rising star in community leadership and people will talk about you in a positive way. Among community leaders, you will become someone they consider a doer and you will be positioned as a genuine leader within the community.

Let's talk about some specific opportunities to serve and to lead in your community.

Volunteer - Help organize an event by serving on the planning committee. If you don't have time for that, simply volunteer to help at the event by working a shift or two. If you can, try and position yourself somewhere where you will meet lots of people - like as a greeter, ticket sales, or bartender.

Appointments - Just about every government agency has opportunities to be appointed to a committee or commission. Local government committees are a critical tool for engaging the public. These positions often go unfilled or have high turnover. Most of the time, the only requirement for appointment is that you be a member of the public and not necessarily have any specific expertise. The best way to find appointment opportunities is to visit the website of your county, city, town, village, school district, or other special district in your community. The other place to look for appointments is your state Governor's office. In most states, the Governor gets to make hundreds of appointments to various advisory committees and commissions. Sometimes these appointments come with a small stipend for attending each meeting.

Elected Office - You may be surprised to learn how many opportunities there are to serve in elected office. The obvious positions are the state legislature, city council, county supervisor, or school board. However, many communities' special districts are governed by an elected board. I have seen elected board positions over water districts, fire districts, park districts, public utilities, and even cemetery districts. Sad to say, but often no one runs for these positions. You can potentially win by simply putting your name on the ballot. To find opportunities to serve in elected office in your community, I recommend visiting your county voter registration/elections office.

Join or Launch a Community Initiative - For me, it all started with a playground. Having recently moved into my community, we took our small children to the neighborhood tot lot. It was nice, but also very basic. I had previously lived in a town with a massive playground. That night I went online and posted in a forum to see if anyone would like to work on a community-built playground initiative. Soon, we organized as a parent group and talked to elementary-age kids about what they would like to see in a new playground. We even had them vote for their preferences by secret ballot! Ultimately, we raised over $300k to purchase the equipment and used sweat equity to build it. This community playground has fundamentally changed our city for the better.

If you see a need that excites you, jump in headfirst to fill that need - don't wait to be asked. You will be amazed by how willing people are to accept new blood. There is just so much work to be done in a community that when someone new comes along and is willing to actually do the work - that person is embraced. If you see a need and no one else is leading the charge to fill it, launch a new program or initiative. Before you know it, people will come along beside you to help. Most people living in a community want to do their part and they just need to know how to get plugged in. That's where you come in.

Jump right in - It is what leaders do!

Step 5 - Building & Maintaining Momentum

Now, imagine that you are attending three to five community events a month, meeting new people constantly, and sitting down with community leaders for coffee three to five times a week. In just a few weeks, the number of meaningful conversations you have with these folks will add up quickly.

---

5 Meetings/Week X **24** Weeks (6 months) =

120 New Community Leader Connections

Your goal is to cultivate these relationships and strengthen them over time - developing a solid working relationship. You also need to continue to meet new people and also cultivate those relationships and develop them. Given the constraint of time, a real question to ask is how can you keep doing more outreach, while also building on the relationships you have just made?

Social media.

Social media is a powerful tool to build and maintain relationships at a large scale. Albeit the relationships won't be as deep as personally cultivated relationships, social media is the perfect tool for achieving your goal of raising your community profile. Sort of like putting people on your bus as it rolls down the road, social media is how you can continue to engage with the people you are meeting along the way. Follow these simple steps and you will build such momentum that key community leaders will take notice and will talk about you and how plugged into the community you are. Remember, people like to rally behind the rising star and social media is a tremendous way to raise your star.

Here some simple tips toward using social media as a community leader.

After you meet each person, follow or like them on social media. I suggest even sending a quick personal note that it was nice to meet them.

Include details of where you met so they can more easily remember you. I think Facebook is the most effective tool to do this. However, LinkedIn and Instagram can also be used effectively.

Divide your social media posts into these buckets:

- **Bucket 1 – Personal.** People want to get to know you personally. Post pictures of your family, outings you go on, praise for your family, your pets, and important life milestones that are meaningful to you. This is where you can highlight your hobbies and interests. But don't get too personal. People don't want to see pictures of your injured foot. If you like to cook, post photos. Maybe you are a runner, a reader, or love coffee. Don't be afraid to let people get to know your personal side.

- **Bucket 2 – Positional.** Think about the elected position you want to serve in or the elected official you want to influence and post items relating to the position. Most government agencies have social media accounts. You can follow and share their events, information, and other key posts. The point of these posts is to position yourself as someone who is active, engaged, and knowledgeable. You will become the perceived expert on the issues relevant to the elected office you are targeting. People will look to you for this important information - much like they expect it from their elected officials. Do this consistently.

- **Bucket 3 – Community.** Use this opportunity to share information about other people and prop up the good work they are doing in the community. If you attend a community event, post a picture of the event (not necessarily a selfie) and give a compliment to the organizers of the event. Or highlight a community leader or organization who is doing amazing things. The key here is that you are focussing on someone or something other than yourself. In doing so, you are communicating to your social network just how deeply woven you are to the civic fabric of your community.

Don't be a one-dimensional poster. People get turned off if all you post is selfies about yourself or photos of your food every day. Your goal should be to rotate postings within the above buckets at a rate of fairly even distribution. Your social media feed should reflect each of the three buckets about one-third of the time.

Post regularly. I recommend that you try and post daily or at least 5 times a week. You all know that person who posts several times a day - about random things. Don't be that person. However, for this strategy to work effectively, you must post consistently and be in the feeds of your new community leader friends.

Don't be too political or partisan. I suggest you pick and choose your social media battles. We all know that person who only talks about their party, their politics, or complains about people in power. Right now, you are raising your profile, with a community-oriented lens and want to appeal to as many people as you can. There is no need to alienate yourself among a fraction of these people you meet.

Don't post anything you wouldn't want your mother (or employer) to see. Social media posts can live forever, often even after you delete them. If you are upset, set your device down, take a walk, and think about whether you would like your post to live forever. Can it be taken out of context or used against you? If so, don't post it.

Remember, the target audience of your social media strategy are the civic insiders of your community - the grasstops leaders whom you are meeting along the way. Your social media strategy is not about voter communication. The average voter doesn't pay attention to important community issues until the last few weeks of a campaign. However, civic insiders pay attention year-round. As you embark on this strategy to raise your community profile, you want to create a positive buzz among the insiders. Done right, they will talk about you and engage directly with you. You will hear statements like, "Have you met Jan? She is everywhere!" Once that happens, you know you are doing it right.

You are working hard to be present in your community and meet new people. Social media is a tool to scale your relationship building and you can use it to maintain and build upon the momentum you are building and stay connected to those you meet along the way.

5

CRAFT YOUR 6-MONTH WORK PLAN

Now it's time to take what you have learned and craft an action plan tailored for you.

First, think about your ultimate goal. Do you want to run for office? If so, which office? If your goal is advocacy and to influence an elected body, what government body is that? Or, maybe your goal is to simply raise your profile in your community in a strategic way to influence issues as they come along.

What is your specific goal?

_____

_____

_____

_____

Next, define the geography of your specific goal. If it's to run for office, then your geographic boundary is the district you hope to be elected in. If it's to influence an elected body, the boundary is the entire government jurisdiction boundary. If it's generally to raise your profile, focus on your immediate community. This is your neighborhood first and city/county next.

Define your targeted geographic boundary.

_____

_____

_____

_____

Who are the grasstops leaders within your targeted boundary? Remember, grasstops leaders are anyone with a title. This list should include elected officials, people appointed to boards and commissions, nonprofit leaders, coaches, pastors, community association presidents, and, really, anyone with a title. To be most effective, try and align this group with your specific goals. Also, include those organizations that align with who you are - based upon our self-identification activity.

Who are your targeted grasstops leaders?

_____

_____

_____

_____

_____

Now, let's take time to do a little research and write down the specific community networking opportunities. These are the community meetings, nonprofit fundraisers, mixers, service club events, town hall meetings, community festivals, and more. Also think about the self-analysis from earlier and identify groups/organizations that align with you. You can find these events on your city/town website, local news sources, Facebook, meetup, and more.

Write down a specific list of community networking events within your targeted geographic boundary.

_____

_____

_____

_____

_____

_____

_____

_____

_____

_____

Now that you have identified the specific community networking opportunities within your targeted area, let's identify when exactly the event will occur and place them in your planning calendar.

After adding these events, use the calendar to also map out when you will meet with which individual grasstops leaders. Be realistic about how many meetings you can have per week in the context of also attending community networking opportunities and put it all on the calendar.

SUN	MON	TUE	WED	THU	FRI	SAT

PRIORITIES

☐ _____
☐ _____
☐ _____
☐ _____
☐ _____
☐ _____
☐ _____

NOTES _____
_____
_____
_____
_____
_____
_____
_____

After a few weeks of attending community networking opportunities and meeting with grasstops community leaders, you will have a sense of what your community needs (deficiencies and opportunities) and what, specifically, you are interested in engaging with. These activities include joining a committee, helping to plan an event, getting appointed to a commission or committee, or launching a new community initiative. Remember, only say yes to something you are genuinely interested in and have the time to commit to seeing through. How you navigate these first couple of leadership opportunities will set the tone for how other grasstops community leaders view you, your potential as a community leader, and your motives.

What specific leadership opportunities or initiatives will you pursue?

_____

_____

_____

_____

_____

_____

_____

_____

6

YOUR ROADMAP TO COMMUNITY LEADERSHIP

Once these worksheets are complete, this is your roadmap for how to go about strategically raising your community profile. As you can see, it isn't rocket science or really that complicated. Why is it then that more people don't go down this path and become leaders in their community? The answer is simple. It takes time, focus, and follow-through - things that most people are not willing to do. We live in a busy world and everyone juggles multiple daily priorities. Those who make their community a priority and do the things outlined in this handbook will be on their path to becoming a community leader.

I told you before that I live in the world of simplicity and common sense. That part is true, and you have likely seen that within the context of this handbook and my style. However, I also live in the world of hard work, strategic thinking, and follow-through. Do these things and not only will you raise your community profile, but you'll also be doing more than 90 percent of the world's population.

5-Step Plan for World Domination

Following my 5-Step Plan for World Domination will facilitate your rise to notoriety within your community. Your network will expand significantly, your base of community support will grow, your profile will rise, and you will become someone who is influential within your community, a grasstops community leader. The biggest question to contemplate at this point will be - What do I want to do with my community leadership role?

Are you interested in running for political office? That is the path I took, and I have no regrets. Serving in elected office is one of the most rewarding endeavors I have ever been a part of.

With an elected position and title, you have great influence. People will listen to you, they'll show up when you ask them to help, and you have a vote that can make the kind of change happen that you want to see happen. You can shape our community along the lines of your vision. There are lots of questions to ask before considering a run for elected office and I want to help you along this journey.

As a political coach, I am here to help you. Helping others to achieve their community leadership goals is my passion as I aspire to help raise up the next generation of community leaders. Please connect with me at www.runforlocaloffice.com and I'll be happy to provide you with my complementary, "10 Key Questions to Ask When Considering a Run for Elected Office."

Maybe running for office isn't your immediate goal, but you picked up this handbook to be a more effective community advocate. The strategies in this handbook will help you immensely. Follow this handbook and you will become a person of influence in your community, building a large and diverse base of support you can now activate around issues of importance to you and your community. Once you do this, you'll naturally identify effective ways to advocate your cause. However, if you are interested in learning strategic advocacy tactics, I am also here to help. Please contact me through my website and let me be your thought partner.

The good news is that you don't have to go at it alone. Please count me as a resource in your journey. If you have questions along the way or want to bounce ideas off of someone, reach out. The strategies laid out in this handbook are not complex, but they work. If you plan and execute aggressively, you can raise your profile in a relatively short while. However, the key to success in the long term is steadiness and consistency. Do these things over a long period and your network will continue to grow and your influence will follow. The key to your success, like anything, is execution.

Show up. Listen. Follow Up. Work Hard. Repeat.

About the Author

Gary Davis has coached over 350 candidates running for local and state office while also serving in three local elected positions, including Mayor, City Council, and School Board. His passion for serving in local office and helping other helping others to get elected is what drove him to write this handbook and develop the Run for Local Office Candidate Coaching Program. For more information, visit him at www.RunforLocalOffice.com

CPSIA information can be obtained
at www.ICGtesting.com
Printed in the USA
LVHW08030718121121
703569LV00014B/974